Teach Kids About Diversity

Why Understanding Cultural Differences, Social Justice, Diversity, Racism, and Equality Is Important for Kids

Frank Dixon

Before we begin, I have something special waiting for you. An action-packed 1 page printout with a few quick & easy tips taken from this book that you can start using today to become a better parent right now!

It's my gift to you, free of cost. Think of it as my way of saying thank you to you for purchasing this book.

Claim your download of Profoundly Positive Parenting with Frank Dixon by scanning the QR code below and join my mailing list.

Sign up below to grab your free copy, print it out and hang it on the fridge!

Sign Up By Scanning The QR Code With Your Phone's Camera To Be Redirected To A Page To Enter Your Email And Receive INSTANT Access To Your Download

Before we jump in, I'd like to express my gratitude. I know this mustn't be the first book you came across and yet you still decided to give it a read. There are numerous courses and guides you could have picked instead that promise to make you an ideal and well-rounded parent while raising your children to be the best they can be.

But for some reason, mine stood out from the rest and this makes me the happiest person on the planet right now. If you stick with it, I promise this will be a worthwhile read.

In the pages that follow, you're going to learn the best parenting skills so that your child can grow to become the best version of themselves and in doing so experience a meaningful understanding of what it means to be an effective parent.

Notable Quotes About Parenting

"Children Must Be Taught How To Think, Not What To Think."

– Margaret Mead

"It's easier to build strong children than to fix broken men [or women]."

- Frederick Douglass

"Truly great friends are hard to find, difficult to leave, and impossible to forget."

– George Randolf

"Nothing in life is to be feared, it is only to be understood. Now is the time to understand more, so that we may fear less."

– Scientist Marie Curie

Table of Contents

Introduction

My dear friend Aristotle was right when he said that man is a social animal. Survival is only possible when we live with harmony, love, and respect for one another. It is only possible when we choose to accept each other's differences—whether they are cultural, sexual, or in our aptitudes—and come together to hold hands and stand for equal rights. It is only possible when we choose love over hate, right over wrong, and truth in the face of everything that's wrong with this world.

It is diversity that makes life so colorful and enigmatic.

Like water, we have our own fluidity. We take the shape of our vessel, whichever it may be. We hope to find our place in the world because we all deserve to be loved, celebrated, and acknowledged. However, in recent times, things have gotten a little messed up, and I wonder if we are leaving a better or worse place for our children to grow up in.

Racial discrimination and a lack of inclusion have made it harder for young people to be themselves. They can't be who they want to be because they fear the world will ridicule them. We stereotype certain ethnicities (one in particular), and they are bombarded with abuse, injustice, and inequality. This may not be the case in your household, but there are many who should be raising better, more sensible adults to inherit the world out there.

In this guide, we talk about diversity and its importance in today's realm. We talk about how it is our duty to raise children who are tolerant and accepting of people of color in their communities. This book talks about patience and inclusion. It talks about the beauty and intelligence that diversity brings to the table.

The Black community has suffered a lot in the past and continues to suffer today. As parents and mentors, we can put an end to this injustice by showing children how to be friends with people of color—how to make them feel included and loved. We can teach them how to advocate for their rights when they are bullied at school or oppressed by unjust laws. We can support them to feel like they are equal.

Let's raise kids to be open-minded. Let's raise them to move ahead and befriend people of color, who have every right to be valued and appreciated. Their efforts deserve to be recognized by us and the world.

We are the ones who can make the difference and ensure that future generations stop judging people by the color of their skin, how they look, or how they want to be identified. Let's start with the former, and then, hopefully, one day, when we live in a world where everyone has equal rights and opportunities, we can peacefully resolve the latter issues.

Chapter 1:

Diversity and Inclusion

Every time we look at our children playing in the mud, trying to do things on their own, learning to repeat back words to us, etc., a thought worries us. They are so unspoiled, pure, and naïve—how will they handle the harsh realities of life as they grow older?

Will they be free to exercise their rights, go out at night alone without the fear of being mugged or harassed, and be given the same opportunities someone of different skin color gets? Will their skills be valued, their opinions heard, and their choices to live life on their own terms appreciated? Or will they have to live in fear, suffer brutality at the hands of the system, and prove themselves and their worth again and again? Will they be bullied for being a darker-skinned kid at school, miss out on opportunities they are equally qualified for, and be looked down upon as if they were criminals?

For any Black parent, these fears are real and perturbing. They live in constant fear that their children will not be considered for things they have worked so hard for and will only be judged by the color of their skin.

It isn't only Black parents who feel this way, though; it is every parent of a child with unique and uncommon traits or identities. Some are judged for practicing their religion, while others have trouble because of their sexuality. Some are physically disabled and need special care, while others are battling mental struggles and disorders.

Every parent whose child would qualify as diverse and different will worry about their child going into the world on their own. As parents, we want to protect them, but how far can we go? We can't be with them in places like classrooms, shopping malls, movie theaters, or friend's houses. We can't always be there to advocate for them and fight for their rights.

So, what is it that we can do?

We start with education: education about the various cultures, ethnicities, races, and religions. We teach our kids how to respect other people's choices to be who they are and what they represent. We can teach them to hold high values and include everyone in the circle without judgment or prejudice. We can instill strong morals that enable them to stand up for those who can't defend themselves to enjoy the same rights and opportunities.

Regardless of where we live, what communities we belong to, or what companies we have joined, it is important to instill tolerance and acceptance for one another within our children. This is how we can have impactful conversations about topics such as diversity and its importance in today's world.

One of the main reasons parents fear having this conversation over the dinner table is because they think that their children are too young for such discussions or because they won't have the answers to all their children's questions. Children, though, aren't colorblind, at least not to race. It is only a matter of time before they are exposed to some racial prejudice in one form or another.

Children start to notice gender and racial differences at the age of two. At three, they can label boy and girl and name the colors of skin. After three, they can notice physical disabilities. By the time they turn five, you can expect them to display gendered behavior. Around the same age, they also become aware and fearful of differences.

Gender and race differences become perceptible as soon as children start to communicate. They may come up with questions about differences of skin color, hair texture, and even social and cultural backgrounds, such as "why does my friend get to celebrate Juneteenth while I can't?"

No matter how young or old your child is, now is the time to have these conversations with them at home. You can teach them how to appreciate diversity and talk about the many amazing things that happen when we do.

Teaching About Diversity–The Need

Nations are diverse, and we are all expected to learn to accept one another and respect our differences. There is so much that we can learn from others' wisdom and experiences. However, on most days, fear and uncertainty prevent us from knocking on our neighbors' doors and asking if their children would like to play. This is particularly true when it comes to racial and cultural differences. As parents, we are in a unique position to engage in conversations that determine what it means to be a child in this diverse world and what role a parent can play to ensure that kids love others and feel loved.

When we say that we want our children to grow up in a free world, we are essentially saying that we want them to reach for their dreams and achieve them. We want them to feel prepared, mentored, and confident. We want them to feel included and valued. We don't want others to reject them or their ideas or to shun their voice and opinions. Still, no matter how hard we try to tell them that the world is entirely filled with love, it isn't. Some people taint the beauty in the world. They set the world on fire by igniting differences among fellow beings based on caste, creed, religion, and race.

As adults, we have all felt a little discriminated against at some point in our lives, and we know how much it hurts. So, how can we want a child to go through the same thing, even when they aren't ours? Children don't deserve to carry those scars into adulthood, thinking they are less than others. This mindset affects their goals, dreams, life choices, and feelings of self-worth.

Therefore, let's talk about diversity more often than before. Let's become pro-diversity and encourage our children to raise their voices against brutality, injustice, and discrimination. Doing so will help them in many ways. For example, they will learn to see all humans as equals and not expect to be treated differently. They will realize that despite our differences, everyone has the right to dress, eat, or celebrate their culture as they like.

Research reveals that children introduced to diversity at a young age have strong social skills (Allen & Kelly, 2015). They are also more receptive of those who speak a different language or have a different skin color. Since all children have a natural willingness to learn, we can immerse them in culturally diverse activities to understand different races and ethnicities better. They can begin by interacting with someone who looks different than themselves at school or in their neighborhood. Increasing their exposure will help normalize these differences and make them see everyone as an equal. This doesn't just apply to extending a hand to people of color but also to those who have a different sexual orientation or physical abilities. This is how we can foster tolerance and patience. Being exposed to people from different races as a start will make children more open-minded and empathetic toward others.

Another study proposes that exposing young children to diversity early on has an impact on how successful they will be as adults (Cesare, 2015). This research was centered around youth of seven countries, aged 4–15. It found that children rejected unfair deals that promoted advantages for some and disadvantages for others. This revealed that they have within them the will to choose right over wrong naturally. We just need to push that message and bring it to light. Imagine if our children were to work with others with commitment and respect, regardless of where they came from, what they look like, or what they represent… Wouldn't that make for an amazing place to be?

How to Get the Conversation Going

Most discussions about diversity and discrimination happen within our educational institutions and in homes when children reach middle and high school. We have decided, though, that young children aren't yet capable of comprehending such complex concepts. Therefore, we delay exposing them to injustices as long as possible. We see evil and we turn our heads away. We fear retribution for becoming involved. How many of us have stopped for a minute, though, to think that many children don't have the luxury of being shielded from evil this way? How many have been exposed to injustices even before they learned to speak?

Besides, why delay, when research has told us that children are naturally compassionate? They have a passion for fairness and demand justice over injustice. They aren't blind to the world around them.

We assume that children will naturally learn to distinguish right from wrong. They will have a positive and sensible outlook toward others as they grow older, so why rush? Again, research suggests otherwise. It proposes that advocating and exposing young children to diversity is beneficial.

Rodolfo Mendoza-Denton who worked on this idea, believes parents who deliberately delay and put off conversations about prejudice and discrimination promote it (Mendoza-Denton, 2011). When children are at a tender age, they notice and reason about differences. However, they don't always respond positively to those observed differences. By the time they turn five, they express preference for their own race (Kinzler & Spelke, 2011).

Another study suggests, on the other hand, that being able to talk to children about race and racism prevents prejudice in them (Aboud & Doyle, 1996). Research by Michelle Lease and Jamilia Blake suggests that when children are friends with other children of different ethnicities, they are more socially skilled (Lease & Blake, 2005).

The concept of diversity, meanwhile, doesn't solely involve conversations about people of color. It also includes conversations about people who speak a different language, are from a different part of the world, or practice a different religion. We have to be tolerant of everyone, and we have to push the message into children's minds instead of letting them figure it out on their own.

Since children pick up most of their habits from their parents, how we look at diversity shapes their minds too. It is hard to change a habit, let alone replace it with a new one. Our comments, opinions, and behaviors around people of different colors and sexual orientations are seen and heard by our children too. If they sense prejudice or privilege, they will take in the same values. This is why it is important to change your mindset first so that you raise a child who is open-minded and willing to share their life with diverse people without feeling ashamed or guilty.

If your child shows interest in seeking clarification about why some people look or dress differently, don't let that opportunity go by. Tomorrow's world is a world of collaboration. More and more companies are expanding their workforce by going offshore or giving chances to people who identify themselves differently. This means that whether you like it or not, your child will have to work with diverse people as they grow up. They will be the outcasts if they are perceived as feeling superior to their coworkers in any sense.

A child's racial beliefs are also heavily influenced by their environment. This means that if your child hangs out with people who don't extend their hands to people of color or those with a different sexual orientation, your child will see that as normalized behavior too. This makes it even more important to start the conversation about race, culture, and ethnicities. Being silent or tiptoeing around the subject won't do any good. It won't stop your child from noticing and picking up subtle behaviors and attitudes.

When children spend most of their time in less diverse environments, their exposure remains limited. This results in fewer conversations about diversity and less engagement with children their own age. This widens the gap and provides more room for prejudice. We have all had similar experiences where our mindset about an individual changed completely when we conversed with them. Sometimes, appearances can be deceiving. It is only when we take the time to fully listen and comprehend the other side of the story that we see the injustice. Inclusion alone develops respect for differences. Active conversation and support, therefore, are important from parents and teachers. This guards against stereotypical thinking and predisposition against other groups.

So, how can we best prepare our kids to meet the challenges that come with collaboration? How can we increase their exposure, build tolerance, and foster patience in them? How can we inspire love and harmony and give all children equal opportunities to strive and succeed? How can we raise them to celebrate diversity instead of viewing it as a nuisance? These are all important questions that we need to ask ourselves so we can raise children who are empathetic and accepting of all cultures, races, sexualities, and disabilities.

Chapter 2:

Beyond White and Black

When African slaves spent their days cooking, cleaning, and getting beaten and lynched for their rich White masters, the White population was being educated. In the 1800s, many schools offered free education for White folks. Despite being born here in the US and having spent their entire lives working tirelessly to give their children a roof over their heads, Black people were denied any right to schooling for centuries. This changed when Abraham Lincoln stepped into office and later signed the Emancipation Proclamation in 1863. This decree was widely seen as promising, but it did little directly and only outlawed slavery in the rebellious southern states. Later came the more significant 13th Amendment in Lincoln's second term, which officially prohibited slavery throughout the U.S. However, it was only enforced after the Civil War, and one can't overlook the fact that White people had hundreds of years of exposure to education in philosophical thought and scientific reasoning, and they had hundreds of years to discover the magic of reading that shaped their dreams into reality, while enslaved Black people were actively discouraged from reading and learning.

The Lincoln administration tried its best to right all wrongs in the education sector. From arranging housing to allowing Black people to own and run their businesses, this was the first time that the U.S. was witnessing the rise of Black businessmen, politicians, churches for Black people, and more. Sadly, the country soon reversed course. In 1865, Lincoln's promises died with him in the theater, and Andrew Johnson took over as the next president. As soon as he stepped into the office, he confiscated the lands given to African Americans in the Lincoln times and gave them back to White southerners.

During this time, some schools for freed slaves emerged. However, their struggle was real, too, as the classrooms were small and the class rosters large. They had no proper stationery, furniture, or desks. The shacks they called their classrooms had leaky ceilings and limited utensils. They received hand-me-down supplies and textbooks from White schools. They had teachers with limited educational backgrounds, and the resources that were gathered for those schools were few and of poor quality. Meanwhile, by the 19th century, 17 states and the District of Columbia demanded school segregation.

This seemed poised to change when in 1952, 13 families from Topeka decided to file a lawsuit against the Board of Education. The families demanded quality education for their children—the kind that the children of White people were receiving. The case received nationwide recognition and came to be known as the *Brown v Board of Education* case. The case was won by the families, which was seen as a great victory for the African American community and students. It gave many Black families hope that their children would no longer have to suffer injustices in the education system and would be taught the skills that would help them excel.

However, the verdict was not welcomed by the White community and sent the nation into a frenzy. Some parents didn't want their children to study in the same school where a 'Negro' was to study. On June 11, 1963, the Governor of Alabama, George Wallace, went as far as to stand in the door of the University so that no Black students could get in to register. It was only when President John F. Kennedy called in the National Guard that he stepped down.

So, those of you who are White parents can imagine the struggle Black children have had to go through just to share the same classroom with your child. It took them years to be recognized as equals in school, and they continue to suffer discrimination at the hands of the teachers and students alike.

The struggles of children with non-heterosexuality are more or less the same as those of minority races. They too have to demand respect from everyone around them. They too are cornered in the hallways, made fun of, and isolated, solely because they are strong enough to accept who they are. This is both sad and hurtful, and the times when we choose to close our eyes to such important issues are the moments when we give them room to recur. When no one raises their voices against the people who make fun of and bully these children, these issues become more ingrained.

Below, you will find a recap of what happens when we turn a blind eye and close our ears so that the chatter doesn't reach us.

What Happens When We Close Our Eyes and Ears

Missed opportunities are one of the most important factors to consider. Many studies propose that Black children are behind White students academically. They do more poorly in standardized tests than White children, which is a testament to the lack of opportunities they receive (Carnoy & García, 2017). Imagine if they received half the opportunities White children enjoy. It's no wonder that we see so few Black people representing the country on international platforms. The consequences of this include:

- Lowering of education outcomes for Black children
- Widening of the performance gap between Black and White children

Trust issues are also common among children of color. They fear abandonment by their White friends. In some states where there is little tolerance toward Black folks, their children are not invited to birthday parties because parents don't want to answer questions from neighbors, friends, and family members. Some parents tell their children to not form any bond, friendship, or romance with Black people, as that would mean increased involvement with them and their families, and the parents don't feel ready for that. Along with this, many Black people suffer economic hardships. They don't have the same kind of luxuries their White friends enjoy, and, therefore, they feel intimidated.

According to one report, it was found that Black children are more likely to be exposed to daunting and threatening experiences in their lives than White children. Systematic inequality continues to haunt them. Being a Black kid on the street is a nightmare for many children. They constantly fear brutality and unwarranted scrutiny from everyone around them. It's like they are watched and judged for every action.

The same is the case with students in schools, where the majority of the kids are from White families. Their skills and learning are questioned. Their ideas are challenged and often overlooked. Their opinions go unheard. They have to be on their A-game all the time to prove that they deserve to be there like any other student—one small blunder, and they have to pay the price. There is little leniency shown.

Poor and limited social skills-building is also an issue and an important one. Black children don't receive the same kind of exposure a White child does. Children who have different sexual orientations similarly have to justify their choices to different people all the time, while children with physical disabilities often try to isolate themselves from the world because it isn't ready for them. When these issues arise and children are denied social inclusiveness, they fail to hone their social skills, such as communication, collaboration, composure, sharing their valuable opinions, and accepting graciously what others have to bring to the table—all important skills.

Lack of confidence is also a given when different children get labeled for all the wrong reasons. They feel uneasy, watched, and ridiculed all the time. They feel there is no safe space for them to express who they are. They are constantly bombarded with questions about why they are different, why they don't act like 'normal' kids, and why they deserve special treatment. Lack of confidence leads to many self-destructive and negative emotions. One becomes cautious of how to act around others. They feel intimidated. They feel that others don't see them as equals. They are asked to step out of line at a public space where everyone else is allowed to go freely. They are asked hurtful questions and scrutinized based on the way they look or dress.

My Skin/Sexual Choices Don't Determine Who I Am—The Beauty of Diversity

There is beauty in diversity. We have to give up on the labels and the detest-filled glares when we are made to stand with an African American in a grocery line. We don't need to hide our purses when we see a Black person walk by. We don't have to leave hateful remarks and comments on social media about people who choose to identify differently than what they were assigned at birth. We have to stop making fun of people with physical disabilities in our social circles.

Not all African American people are thieves. Not all people with a different sexual preference are out of their minds and have fallen away from religion. Not all those with a physical disability chose to have it. Above all, they are people like you and me with every right to breathe the same fresh air we breathe. We must value human lives. We must set aside our political affiliations for a moment and think about how we are feeding into this whole culture. Are we portraying a promising and harmonious image? Are we setting the right example for our children to follow?

Everyone has an equal right to live their life in harmony without being stereotyped and looked down upon. We have to stop hurting their feelings and show remorse.

We have to stop pretending like they don't matter, because they do. We all do!

We all have the power to change the world for the better. Each one of us! It is time we take this responsibility seriously and do what's right by everyone. No one should be above or below the law. There shouldn't be any distinction between the rich and the poor. At the end of the day, we all stand in the same line at a shop. No one gets treated as a priority.

Just as you wouldn't want your child to come home crying on the first day of school because no one wanted to sit with them at lunch in the cafeteria, other parents don't want their children to feel the same way. Children and adults, no matter the color of their skin, deserve to be respected. They deserve to be treated as equals because, before every other right that the law gives them, it is the human rights that they are entitled to—to be considered as humans and beautiful ones.

Who can say what they aren't capable of if given the same opportunities as White people? If they are given the same chances, they won't have to engage in earning money illegally. If they were given the same opportunities, systematic injustice wouldn't be an issue to worry about.

No George Floyds would have to die in police custody due to police suspicion toward Black people running so deep. No one from the LGBTQ+ community would commit suicide because the people around them can't accept them for who they are, something that is genetic and therefore outside of their control. It is a proven statistic that children aged 12–14 who classify themselves as bisexual, transgender, lesbian, or gay are six times more likely to commit suicide than heterosexual teenagers of the same age (Ream, 2019). If only we were to give them some space to be whoever they are, the deaths would be fewer.

Now is the time to think about what we have been doing wrong and how we plan to change. Start by developing compassion and acceptance toward people of a different race, ability, and sexual orientation—we have to raise a generation that knows how to celebrate these differences and include people from all spheres of life with open hearts and arms.

Chapter 3:

We Are All Different but the Same

We all come from different backgrounds, have had different experiences growing up, and have different interests and hobbies—all of which shape our personalities. Even children growing up in the same household can hold different values and ideas. One may be kind and empathetic, helping injured birds so that they can fly again, while the other has no sympathy and loves to walk over the army of ants in the garden every day. We know who is behaving well and who isn't, yet we don't tell the 'bad' ones to leave the house. Instead, we mold them, guide them, and make them feel like part of the family. We don't isolate them or leave them to deal with their problems on their own. We work with them to help them to strive and succeed.

If we can change their mindset to become humble and understanding, why can't we change our own? Why can't we show empathy for the people who look or act differently? Why can't we be less judgmental of others' choices to live their lives on their terms? Why can't we be more accepting of what another person represents or wants to be associated with?

Diversity brings together two different sets of skills, wisdom, expertise, and knowledge. Different experiences garner different opinions and viewpoints. Diversity allows us to view things from a new lens and become more enlightened about the struggles and hardships of others. This isn't just about African Americans; it is also about those in our community who speak a different language. We can't shun them because they are a part of us. Only when we work together can we achieve big things and flourish.

Take the example of your workplace. You must have people of a different race, sexual orientation, or cultural values in your office. How does their unique set of skills come in handy when you have a project to work on? Isn't it every company's goal to outperform competitors and use its resources to the best of its means? This is only possible when every employee gives their best shot and takes a stand for the company whenever needed.

Having people from different backgrounds helps you to view a situation from many angles, especially when you are trying to cater to a larger audience. A diverse workforce can help you tap into different markets, different customers, and different cultures. There is a reason why many U.S. companies advertise and celebrate different festivities like Diwali, Eid, and the Festival of Lights. This is because they want to attract a wider audience living in the States and become a potential seller.

With diversity on its side, any company has a better chance at finding complex solutions in less time. With the experience, wisdom, and intellect of people from different backgrounds, a company stands a better chance at success.

Teaching young minds to appreciate, accept, and celebrate diversity will help them become better versions of themselves. With collaborative efforts, they can then overcome hurdles and challenging times together and excel at whatever they put their minds to.

This is only possible when they first acknowledge their differences and accept them.

Acceptance Comes From Within

Acceptance isn't a simple emotion; it is a willingness to see things as they are. When we say we accept something, we have a general idea of what it means. It means that we are ready to accept who we are, what our financial circumstances are, whether we are happy/unhappy with our job or relationship, etc. Acceptance happens when we stop trying to change things and realize that they are out of our control. We stop wasting our time and energy and let things go.

In psychological terms, acceptance means taking a stance of non-judgmental awareness and embracing the experiences of thoughts, bodily sensations, and feelings as they occur.

The first attribute is becoming non-judgmental, followed by a complete and active awareness of the experiences one feels. One of the key ideas involved in this concept is that no matter how much we try, some realities are inescapable. We can refuse to acknowledge them, but that doesn't do any good. For example, refusing to feel pain won't make it go away. The process of healing begins with acceptance.

The same is the case with diversity. We may not like someone or want to be friends with them. However, that doesn't change the fact that we shall continue to see them every day. There is no escaping or ignoring that. The only way to bridge the gap is through acknowledgment and acceptance. For most people who happen to hold a grudge against someone, acceptance doesn't come easy. We are all filled with emotions, and most of the time, it is these emotions that guide our actions and behaviors. There are only two ways to deal with them: Either accept them or resist them. For many of us, resistance is a default reaction. We hate everything that isn't pleasant to the eyes, ears, or mind. Still, resistance causes more damage than good, according to researchers. One becomes a victim of their own mindset and can't escape.

Before we go any further, we need to understand what acceptance *isn't.* Acceptance isn't an agreement. You may not agree with how things turned out, but you have to live with the consequences. There is no point in struggling against it. Acceptance is also not acquiescence that what happened was right. The world can be a cruel and unjust place, and there is little that we can do to change that. Acceptance isn't about giving up either. It isn't a weakness. It takes real guts, for instance, to admit that you were wrong and show a willingness to change. Finally, acceptance isn't about quitting. It is about shifting your perspective and viewing things differently.

Therefore, to accept others and respect them for their diversity and uniqueness requires open-mindedness. You must understand that there is value in everyone's thoughts. It is easier to find and accept the truth when one is open-minded.

One of the best ways to ensure that you accept and appreciate diversity is via validation. Validation allows others to feel like they belong with you. It strengthens your bond. It is the official language of acceptance. When you validate someone's ideology and perspective, you acknowledge their internal experiences and foster an aura of harmony and peace. It doesn't remain a war any longer. Even if you disagree with their ideals, you accept and respect them for it.

As the world becomes more interconnected and diverse, comprehending and validating different cultures, people, and their journeys becomes crucial. Without showing acknowledgment of their beliefs and why you respect them, you can never be a good role model for your children, who look up to you to seek more clarity about diversification. By accepting these differences, you can create a safe place for them to question and argue. By understanding cultural differences, you can consider the context of why some people act and live differently than you, why they have different social identities, and what historical struggles they have overcome to be where they are today.

Acceptance—The First Step to Appreciating Differences

The more important question is: How do you cultivate acceptance toward people of different races, ethnicities, cultures, and sexual preferences in your children? You begin by questioning your patterns. Why do you feel hatred or disgust toward someone? What harm have they caused you? Have you formed a general perception about someone, or have you actually had a bad experience with them firsthand?

As it turns out, most of the time, our behaviors and actions stem from what we have been told and trained to do our whole life. I believe the education sector has a key role to play here. In my classroom, we were told that same-sex relations are a pestilence, and those involved are doomed to go to hell because they didn't conform to the ideals set by the Almighty. We were reminded to not engage with those involved or form friendships with them because that would make us sinners too. There was no explanation as to why God wanted us to refrain from forming a bond with our fellow humans. We were just told to blindly follow the agenda without reasoning, and most of us did. We carried those lessons in our hearts and minds for several years until we finally had an awakening about how wrong those lessons were. How can you move forward in life if you stick with your old beliefs and resist changing with time?

Did you know there is evidence that the most horrendous terrorist attack on American soil could have been prevented, had there been more technical and intelligence personnel to intercept and decipher the messages between the terrorists? Did you know one of the biggest reasons why there was a lack of personnel was because state laws didn't allow people of diverse cultures and sexual orientations to become a part of law enforcement? Even today, many highly competent people from diverse backgrounds and races are denied positions they are qualified for because the employers worry it would not sit well with the majority of their employees.

Therefore, we need to question why we can't stand people from different backgrounds. We need to go deeper and understand why these patterns exist. It is best if you write down some of your reflections and look at them with reason. Maybe you have nothing against other people after all. Alternatively, maybe you can turn a new leaf and change how you perceive them.

Challenge the definition of the word 'normal.' We treat people differently because they are viewed as 'other.' There is no universal standard of being normal, though. We are all different and have different interests and qualities. It is our uniqueness that makes us stand out. How can we define ourselves as normal and others as abnormal? There is no scale to measure that.

So, the next time your child comes up to you saying they met someone weird today, ask them to explain what they mean by that. Carefully listen to the description and aim to find out the similarities and differences in that person. Point out what they have in common with the 'weird' person they met and help them see that they aren't that different from us.

Make use of literature and movies to normalize other groups. The next time your children come up to you asking why someone looks different, talk to them about what makes them different, their history, cultural values, and traditions. Use media and literature to your advantage and share stories about your experiences with people who looked different. They will be surprised when you share how different life was for people before them and how badly they were treated by everyone around them. Take Rosa Parks, for example.

Increase their exposure by helping them meet someone different than them. Hearing about that person's struggles firsthand will give the children a better idea of how challenging their life has been because they were perceived as being different. This type of exposure will increase a child's acceptance of diverse people, and they will be more willing to engage and become friends with them.

Use facts. Several documentaries discuss the history and origin of various cultures and sexual orientations. If your child is old enough to see and understand, there is no better way to go about it. When they have the facts and information to go with it, it will become easier to reject stereotypes and the myths that revolve around them. For instance, learning about Black history and why it's important to acknowledge will clear many misconceptions from their minds.

Chapter 4:

Love Is Love–Be Tolerant

Children aren't born with hate for others in their minds. Intolerance is a learned emotion. For the most part, children are empathic, caring, and tolerant. When conversations are never planned or opportunities taken to talk about and introduce young kids to different religions, cultures, and races, though, intolerance breeds in their minds.

It is never too late to begin. The sooner you start having these important conversations about what's happening in the country and how they can choose to not be a part of the hate crimes, the better their chances of developing a tolerant and patient mindset become.

If you want them to have any chance of living harmoniously in this multicultural, diverse, global world, you have to raise them to be tolerant and kind toward others. They should make others feel included. They should voice their concerns regarding hateful agendas with confidence and stand with the victims who have suffered at the hands of the state and dogmatic people for many years.

As patience is a virtue, we can all develop it. It is a skill that can be learned, honed, and mastered. Again, tolerance doesn't mean you accept what the other person has to say—it simply means that you are mature enough to not argue or fight. Having patience means you can calmly wait in the face of adversity and frustration.

We are surrounded by people from different cultures and origins left, right, and center. We can't ignore their existence. We can't debate their inclusion. They have every right to enjoy life as lawful citizens however they like.

So, when we teach children to be patient in other areas of their lives, why can't we make them pro-diversity? In this chapter, we will talk about the need for tolerance in the current time, given the world we are living in. We will emphasize why it's more important than ever to raise patient, well-mannered, and tolerant adults and how to get started.

The Importance of Raising Patient, Well-Mannered, and Respectful Kids

Why be patient and tolerant of others, your child may ask. Well, research reveals that patient people tend to be more empathetic, cooperative, equitable, and forgiving (Schnitker & Emmons, 2007). They allow others to live with their values and traditions in harmony without questioning or judging their ways. They make it possible for others to feel comfortable and safe around them. They don't lose their temper or voice hurtful remarks. They don't blame others and engage in hateful crimes because they need a scapegoat to vent their negative emotions and validate their negative experiences. They don't hold grudges or hold anyone accountable for something they didn't do. They don't give in to hateful agendas propagated through media outlets and newspapers. They know that doing good always comes back as a benefit.

In relationships, patience is an act of kindness. It's your partner comforting you after a bad day at work. It's a child smiling at you for making weird faces. It's an old friend lending you a shoulder to cry on day after day because you couldn't get over heartache.

Patience involves the empathetic assumption that involves alleviating the suffering of those around us, despite having our own personal discomfort (Comer & Sekerka, 2014). This was further explored in an experiment where patients were asked to contribute money into a common pot (Curry et al., 2008). The money was to be doubled and redistributed. The researchers also added an incentive for anyone who would be stingy. Despite the incentive, patient people contributed more to the pot than other people. This revealed that patience is a form of selflessness and agreeableness, a trait that is characterized by cooperation, kindness, and warmth. Patient people, according to research, also tend to be less lonely because they are always making friends with everyone they meet without prejudice or judgment. They are well-equipped to tolerate others' flaws and display more generosity, mercy, compassion, and forgiveness.

Becoming Patient—Getting Started

To become more patient and tolerant toward diversity, you need to first identify the source of your hatred and educate yourself. How do you plan to tackle your impatience? What ticks you off? Once you can pinpoint the cause and effect, you can begin asking yourself some important questions:

- If I still feel uneasy and impatient, how can I handle my reactions better?
- How can my thoughts be more positive and accepting toward diverse people?
- Can my annoyance be channeled elsewhere?
- Can the outcome be in my favor if I stop being annoyed by every little thing?

Next, you need to confront your outdated beliefs. Start by reflecting on your childhood experiences and upbringing. Was your house a source of negativity? Did your parents not see diverse people as equals? Were you told to avoid befriending them because they were different from you?

Sometimes, parents project obsolete ideas into the minds of their children without reason. Now is the time to make a conscious attempt to analyze those concepts and how they have become obsolete today.

Counter prejudiced beliefs. If you hear your child make a prejudiced comment or remark about someone, ask them why they think that way. Once you listen to their reasoning, gently challenge their views by talking about the struggles that person might have faced and how your child's opinion hurts them. For example, if your child says something like, "Black children shouldn't be allowed in playgrounds," ask them why they think that and explain why all children have every right to enjoy their childhood.

Model patience. Are you setting the right standards for your child to follow? Do they find your behavior appropriate and justified? Whatever your thoughts and attitudes are toward people of color and different sexual orientations, remember that your little one is closely noticing it, so set an example that you would be proud of, should they imitate you.

Encourage openness and curiosity. Some parents like to have everything planned out for their children. From what schools their children attend, to what extracurricular activities they partake in, they take pride in being smart parents. If they want their children to respect diversity, then, they should have a similar mindset, starting early and adopting a conviction to raise them accordingly.

Cultivate a sense of pride in your own culture. Show your children why festivals and celebrating them matter to you. Connect them with their heritage and develop an appreciation and respect for your own values and traditions. When children can also garner respect and appreciation for their values, they will learn to hold the values of others in high esteem too. When a child learns to find joy in their own culture and traditions, it becomes easier for them to find joy in the differences of others, say Mary Ann French and Barbara Mathias in their book, *40 Ways to Raise a Nonracist Child* (1996).

Embrace diversity from an early age. This can be achieved when you expose kids to positive images, literature, toys, videos, public role models, and newspaper reports that represent diversity at its best. Encourage them to befriend people who look and dress differently from them without hesitation. Have conversations with them about their cultures and values.

Discourage discriminatory comments. When you see or hear someone making derogatory remarks about someone different, raise your voice against it. Verbalizing your displeasure and letting the individual making those comments know how unappreciative you are of their mindset is the least you can do to make a difference. Let it be known loud and clear that you won't tolerate such prejudice against anyone, and threaten to call the police if they don't back down. Doing so will help resolve an otherwise intensifying and unwanted debate. If you notice a derogatory comment coming from your child, let them know that you won't tolerate this type of biased thinking in your house.

Chapter 5:

Fighting the Hate–What Can I Do?

Not long ago, there was a presidential candidate who won after condescending toward Muslims, Mexicans, Latino women, and people with disabilities.

Not long ago, you could watch as a Muslim woman enjoying her tea in a café was met with another woman screaming anti-Muslim epithets at her. A White male opened fire in a church in Charleston and killed nine African Americans who welcomed him to study in the church. He told the victims he had to do it while killing them. Anti-Semitic graffiti appears in an elementary school in Stapleton, Colorado. A lone and mentally disturbed gunman carried an assault rifle and a handgun while storming a gay club in Orlando, injuring 53 people and killing 49.

Bias is a human condition, and sadly, American history is rife with prejudice against everyone who looks, identifies, and practices religion differently. There has been little tolerance toward diverse people and how they choose to live their lives. Regardless of the progress we have made, stereotyping is still a prevalent issue without any permanent treatment.

When bias stimulates an unlawful act, it becomes a hate crime. Most of these crimes are inspired by religion and race. Hate crimes, in recent times, have been rising, per reports from the FBI. After the spread of COVID-19, people of Asian descent have become a target for bullying. Many had to flee to their home countries, worried about their safety. Not long ago, there was the history-defining case of George Floyd, who died at the hands of police after he was arrested and subdued. Although he had committed a crime, the type of treatment he received wasn't justified.

If you remember the case of Timothy James McVeigh—who bombed one-third of the Alfred P. Murrah Federal Building, injuring 680 people and killing 168 people, 19 of whom were kids—that kind of terrorism was more worthy of death by a knee, and yet, he was arrested rather casually when driving on a highway without a license plate and with an illegal firearm. Also, there was the case of the Milwaukee Cannibal, serial killer and sex offender Jeffrey Dahmer, who was arrested for the murder and dismemberment of 17 men and boys. You can notice the differences in the treatment of criminals with far worse track records than that of George Floyd.

The uproar that followed George Floyd's murder was remarkable, though it wasn't without victims of its own. Shops were looted and property damaged during riots. Police brutality came to the forefront of national discourse as many people came forward to share their stories and horrific experiences at the hands of the state.

When all this happens, it tears communities apart. People are made to choose a side, to break up with their friends and partners because it becomes too much for them to handle. These hate crimes often start on online platforms but can escalate into actual crimes quickly. Many of these hate crimes don't get reported because the victims strongly feel they will be blamed and punished. Many law enforcement personnel are not trained or ready to investigate hate crimes.

Where does that leave you as an individual? How can you play your part in fighting hate speech? What can you do as a citizen of your country to ensure that these things don't happen in your community and workplace?

Where to Start

Standing up to promote tolerance and patience isn't as hard as you may think. As soon as you realize that inclusion and a sense of belonging is everyone's right, you learn to appreciate differences and voice your concerns when you see an unjust incident unfolding.

The good news: You are not alone. It has long been observed that whenever hatred flares up, there are many good people who rise against it. This was most recently exhibited during the Black Lives Matter movement. The world came together, raised their voices, and stood with the Black community. Their stories and experiences were shared worldwide on the news, often sponsored by White folks. People of color received heartfelt condolences from everyone around the globe.

So, don't worry if you think you are the only one who is pro-diversity. Sooner or later, more people will join the cause and raise their voices with you. If you are met with a hate crime, here's what you should do:

Act. Do something in the face of contempt and hatred. If you don't raise your voice, perpetrators will view your apathy as acceptance. This will further challenge the lives and choices of the victims. Hate only persists when we don't take action. You must act, because hate is an open attack on acceptance and tolerance. The best way to counter hate crimes is through acts of goodness. Sitting at your desk won't do your partner any good if they are being attacked. Doing something, however, will.

Silence is deadly and considered validation. You don't want the perpetrator to sense that. Hate crimes are an attack on any community's mental and physical health. When hate crimes against a community become common, the people of that community have no means of escape. They feel isolated, taken advantage of, and victimized. Their mental peace takes a hit; they are worried for their safety and the safety of their families.

They lose their jobs, fall behind on rent and utilities, and suffer socially.

Hate also escalates like fire. Just a simple act of name-calling can turn into a full-blown argument and fight in no time. People have stressed lives, and sometimes, the wrong things become an outlet for release. When this happens, people forget who they are and turn into these vicious, venom-spitting animals with no respect for one another.

When this happens, the first thing you need to do is pick up the phone and call for backup. You don't want to be alone when everyone is triggered. Call a friend or the police if you sense that things are becoming violent.

Afterward, don't forget to speak out about the incident with people you meet in your neighborhood and community. Draft some solutions to prevent a future face-off and see how to calm both heated parties.

You can also sign a petition that you stand against violence as a community and would appreciate it if no such thing happens again. If you are part of a church group, make sure to bring up the topic and lead a prayer to prevent hate crimes from being committed.

If there has been an act of hate-fueled vandalism in your neighborhood, join together to repair it with a message of love and brotherhood.

Support the victims. Your goal should be to report any incident in detail and ask for help. Show support when you learn about a hate crime in your area. This will tell the victims that they have someone to count on. Surround them with protection and comfort.

Victims of hate crime feel afraid and alone. They are attacked for being themselves, for their sexuality, ethnicity, and disabilities. When *we* choose silence, we amplify their isolation. They feel alone and unsupported. Let them know, though, that you are always there to help.

Since most victims of hate crimes fear the system, they will likely choose to let the incident go by. However, they won't forget about it any time soon. Being with them and encouraging them to go to the station or courthouse is one way of showing support. You can get them connected with a lawyer or organization that works for their community if they don't have the means to afford one. You can also go with them to the station and have their report filled out and registered.

As for your children, be aware of the type of exposure they receive: What books they are reading, what media they are exposed to, what curriculum is promoted in their school, etc. Question them about their opinions on people of color and people from the LGBTQ community. Do they seem prejudiced?

Expose your children to multicultural experiences. You can set up a small party for a friend who comes from a different background at your house to celebrate their culture. For example, you can organize a Diwali event for someone of Hindu heritage. This will help normalize friendships with people from diverse backgrounds and encourage your community to join hands with them.

Teach your children to become active advocates for others. Promote taking a stand against bullies. Tell them to report anything wrong. Make sure that they don't remain silent and are confident enough to raise their voice for their friends and classmates when they are treated poorly.

Chapter 6:

Bigotry—It Starts at Home

Sometimes, we are the reason a specific race or culture experiences hatred. We don't do it intentionally, but we also don't make any effort to prove that we're against it. For example, when you go to a bookshop, you unintentionally encourage your child to pick a book with a White child on its cover. When it comes to movie nights, you prefer to watch one with White actors or heterosexual couples. You put parental controls on Netflix so that your child doesn't watch a show or movie with bisexual, transgender, gay, and lesbian couples and storylines.

Maybe you do it because you don't want your child getting confused or you are assuming that they are too young for such exposure, but they aren't blind. They see LGBT couples when they are at the grocery store with you. They witness police brutality and unfairness to African Americans. They see others making fun of people with disabilities or taking advantage of them by parking their cars in their designated spots at restaurants and stores.

They also see *you* not raising your voice in those moments. Your silence gives them the impression that it is wrong to speak up in the moments when you should be modeling the opposite.

It isn't just your silence that causes this shift in their mindset, though; it is your noise too. If you are too loud about your negative views about other communities and people, your children see that. They see you being judgmental and hardhearted. They then feel they have the right to treat people the same way, and their confidence makes them next-generation bullies. Your opinions about people of color, different sexualities, and disabilities speak volumes about how you are raising your child. If you are not careful, you are giving them the right to abuse their power and privilege. You are giving them the right to antagonize others and start a fight. You are making them haters of a certain caste, community, or culture.

How Being Judgmental Affects Your Child

Are you a judgmental parent? Are you a perfectionist who doesn't want to hear an opinion that doesn't resonate with the one you hold? Do you have unrealistic expectations and want everyone to follow the rules and regulations you set? Are you reluctant when discussing issues of race, culture, sexuality, and disabilities with your child? Do you have a controlling attitude? Do you openly judge and ridicule the perspectives of your children, discouraging further arguments? Do you have the habit of bringing down your child's confidence by using words like 'wrong' and 'bad'?

How you see the world affects the way your child sees it. Being exposed to hatred and dislike toward diversity raises them to become haters too. Children look up to us as their role models. They take after our habits and behaviors because they feel we are the best source of information there is. They see how we react and respond to situations and the people creating them and learn to behave in the same manner.

This can be a plus if you are compassionate, appreciative, and pro-diversity. Your children will take after you, holding the same values of affection, encouragement, and appreciation toward people of color, LGBTQ+ communities, and people with physical disabilities. They don't view them as 'others,' and they have the same amount of respect in their hearts as they would have for anyone who resembles them.

Being judgmental, in contrast, affects not only the relationship you have with your child but also their emotional and mental health. When they feel that they can never see eye-to-eye with you on social issues, they feel isolated. When their opinions are labeled childish because they haven't seen the world out there, they feel cornered and invalidated. They feel emotionally insecure because they don't have your support. Your constant reminders of how naïve and impatient they are about supporting social causes sets them back. They feel that your love is conditional. They feel that you will only love them if they act like the puppet you want them to be. They feel they fail to live up to the standards and expectations you have set for them. They feel judged for their choices, and their mind fills with negative thoughts about you. They think twice before coming to you for advice or assistance.

Surely, you don't want that type of a relationship with them, now do you?

Becoming a Torch Bearer

One of the biggest challenges many parents face in this multicolored, stereotyping, and energized world is finding how to help children maintain an open-minded attitude. An open-minded attitude includes acceptance of everyone and their choices, appreciation for differences that are unique to everyone, and the patience to listen and respond, not simply react. Snap judgments, social pigeon-holing, and arbitrary thinking often get in the way, but training kids to take after your good values and ethics isn't difficult. They can learn to not reject anything they disagree with and to calmly listen instead. They can learn about the dangers of narrow-mindedness and how it affects the lives of everyone around them. They can build tolerance by being open to change and new information. They can learn to live in harmony and peace with people from all walks of life. They can take charge and become social activists standing against those who take away others' free will.

Learning about tolerance and non-judgment begins at home. Parents who disclose their social prejudices implicitly encourage young children to follow in their footsteps. Speaking negatively about someone just because they choose to live their life differently, hold different ideals, or practice different religions is misleading and a bad example to set. In doing so, you highlight the differences and perceived flaws in them instead of what makes them human. This prevents your child from leading an open-minded life. They flee from all important discussions about race, ethnicity, and culture because they fear becoming a social outlaw.

Social tolerance can be imparted, though, if parents express appreciation for others and their good intentions, make allowances for oversights and mistakes, and help children educate themselves on the important issues.

Therefore, you must think before labeling something as bad. We are quick to judge because familiarity feels safe, but change isn't always bad. Anything new isn't always bad or unsafe territory. It is simply something that needs more exploration and research on our part. Thanks to the internet, this is easy. Instead of calling things bad, you can say this instead: "This is different from what I have been told, and I need to research this." You can even say something like, "I am not sure how I feel about this issue, but I bet some research will clear my head." This way, children won't fear newness and exploration. They will become more curious, ready to explore more avenues, which may mean talking about an issue with someone with expertise.

Remind your child that there is always more than meets the eye. There are two sides of every coin, and one must not form strong judgments or pass accusations unless one is certain of their opinions. It is best to investigate and research before going into a heated debate with anyone. Hearing both sides of the story might help you form a better judgment and present your case in a manner that doesn't offend the other person.

Encourage big-picture thinking. Broaden a child's view of others by discussing what led them here, what their circumstances are, what personality factors shape their decisions, and what hidden motives they might have for acting in a certain way. Model forgiveness and kindness by asking others to consider charitable and benign explanations when someone behaves aggressively.

Finally, point out the long-term effects of hatred and disgust and how they can lead to an increase in hate crimes. Don't hesitate to be open about how they can affect someone's life and mental state. Being judgmental is easy, but if they can roleplay being on the other side, they will experience how it feels to be singled out and bullied. Assure them that they can always change and question their belief system if they feel it is biased. Assure them that it is safe to raise their voice when they witness injustice at play.

Chapter 7:

Raising a Young Advocate

Have you ever stopped to think about what causes us to act out irrationally? Where does our hatred stem from? Why do we label people as bad or wrong? We judge people because we believe that their choices are against the socially acceptable norms of society, but who really is setting these norms? Who is following them blindly? Why can't we have an opinion that doesn't conform to what society thinks? Why do we have to try and fit everything in a little box?

It is because we have a lack of education, compassion, and understanding of many cultures, subjects, and beliefs. We remain stuck to the mindset we developed when we were young, but that was a different age and time. People did name-call back then, but hate crimes weren't as common as they are today. Today, it only takes a ten-second video to reach out to the world and share an experience—good or bad. Earlier, you had to file a report, bring witnesses, and fight a long court battle to prove that injustice happened. Today, achieving justice is easier than ever.

Let us pass a positive message on to our children and help them advocate for their rights and the rights of others. Let them rise as social advocates who can put an end to unnecessary bullying at school, in public places, and in playgrounds. Teach them how to join hands with people from different communities and become a single voice. This is achievable if we take a stand and point it out when something wrong happens. All it takes is some guts and some mental training to raise children who are responsible, socially just, and compassionate.

How Speaking Up Is Our Ultimate Weapon

Did you know that, according to the National Center for Educational Statistics, many students at schools are bullied over their physical appearance, race, gender, disability, sexual orientation, and religion (Seldin & Yanez, 2019)? Researchers believe that students with physical disabilities are more worried about their safety and being harassed by their peers than students without disabilities (Saylor & Leach, 2008). Race-fueled bullying is also a major cause of concern, as statistics reveal that it damages one's emotional and physical health alike (Rosenthal et al., 2013).

Approximately 23% of African American, 23% of Caucasian, 7% of Asian, and 16% of Hispanic students are bullied at schools. Additionally 70.1% of LGBTQ students are bullied verbally because of their sexual orientation and 59% because of their gender expression. Of these, 28.9% of LGBTQ students were physically pushed and shoved (Kosciw et al., 2018). These are shocking numbers, and only compiled two years ago. The abuse and bullying continue to haunt many children who identify themselves outside the heteronormative construct.

If we want our children to report peer bullying, we need to guide them to bring their petition to the administration. We need to keep in contact with the school administration to see how it is handling the complaint and see if any real change is evident.

One of the stupidest questions that lawyers and school administrators post to the victim concerns whether they changed schools. Think about how stupid that notion is for a minute. If I get robbed twice, will I be asked by the judge to move houses, or will they try to arrest the robbers? Expecting the victim to leave a situation when they are being bullied is nonsensical and it blames them.

We need to change these questions and put more pressure on the administration to introduce bullying-prevention programs. There should also be strict checks against bullies who continue to scare and harass their peers. Since we can't be with our children at school at all times to ensure that the appropriate authorities address harassment, we can teach them some strategies to counter bullying. This way, we can raise them to be thoughtful and engaged and make them a part of positive social change.

Teaching Kids to Advocate for Themselves and Others

We are raising children in an ever-so-connected world where social media influences their thoughts and emotions and drives their actions. We can channel its power to help our children become more aware of what's happening around them and how they can contribute to it positively. When we say that we must raise them to become social advocates for change, we mean that they should remain in the forefront, carrying out their social and humanitarian duties with pride and honor. As a nation, we need to learn to protect our people, no matter what their background or sexual preference is. We need to raise our voices in support of them so that they can feel included and validated.

We must teach children to think critically and view every situation without judgment and bias. We must model respect for one another, especially when there is a difference of opinion. We must fuel kids' curiosity to know more about people from various walks of life and what makes them unique.

For this, you must ask open-ended questions to know what's going on in their minds regarding current issues. You can ask them to share their opinion about what they have to say about a certain piece of news. Ask how it makes them feel. How do they view the whole situation? Who is to blame, etc.? This is a great way to have critical but pivotal conversations while allowing them to express themselves.

If a child has different political views, they should not fear sharing them with their parents. This calls for active listening and empathy. Your child should feel free to present their opinions in a direct and composed manner. Engaging kids in political discourse leads to more clarity about what's morally right and what isn't. If their opinions sound too biased and prejudiced, you can always gently express how you feel about it and how you wish they would do more research before being this blunt and naïve.

To raise socially curious and active children, though, don't flatly disregard their ill-formed opinions. Instead, encourage more thoughtfulness and engagement. The best way to do so is to seek role models they can meet and converse with. When a child notices a gap between a problem and action taken to resolve it, engaging with people with better knowledge and experience is an excellent way to help them grow their knowledge base and hear the other side of the story.

If they want to take up a problem with the school management, help them draw up a draft and encourage taking action. You can get involved by talking to the management about it and seeing what they plan to do about the proposal.

Finally, look for teachable moments. No matter how young or old your child is, there is always room for growth and patience. They can be the torch bearers after you if you model honesty and respect for others. If you catch them standing up for someone, encourage and appreciate them. Discuss what else they could have done and how they could have dealt with the situation, had it gotten worse. Preparing them to plan and to be ready to face backlash and aggression is another way to keep them safe. Usually, advocates are the first ones to get the ax when it comes to a confrontation. If they raise their voice for others and speak about their concerns, they should also know how to handle situations to prevent them from getting out of control.

Conclusion

Learning about diversity and how it helps nations flourish and evolve is an essential parenting requirement. With the way current events are unfolding, we can't leave our children to stay in the dark and not know what's happening around them. Children are naturally kind and compassionate. They aren't born to hate, and, therefore, their ideas about diversity should be positive. However, this isn't always the case, which makes us think about who is raising them and how.

As parents, we need to prepare them to collaborate and work together. At the rate the world is evolving, sooner or later, they will be made to work in an environment that is diverse. We have to play a key role in shaping a positive personality that isn't judgmental, biased, and prejudiced. We need to raise them as leaders who will take everyone forward with them. We have to raise them to be respectful and acceptable toward people who are different. This includes everyone from African Americans to the LGBTQ+ community and people with physical and learning disabilities. We must show appreciation and tolerance for the way they lead their lives without looking down on them. We must graciously open our homes and social circles to them, so they feel included and happy.

In this guide, we have talked about every hurdle that comes along the way and taken a look at how we can overcome them. We have given you the tools and advice to raise an adult who can stand against bullying, bias, and injustice, someone who can say 'no' and support the victim, someone everyone can count on—someone they can trust and be friends with.

Thank you for giving this book a read. I hope you loved reading it as much as I enjoyed writing it. It would make me the happiest person on earth if you would take a moment to leave an honest review. All you have to do is visit the site where you purchased this book: It's that simple! The review doesn't have to be a full-fledged paragraph; a few words will do. Your few words will help others decide if this is what they should be reading as well. Thank you in advance, and best of luck with your parenting adventures. Every moment is a joyous one with a child.

References

5 ways to teach your students to appreciate our differences. (2020, March 12). PLS Classes. https://plsclasses.com/five-ways-to-teach-your-students-to-appreciate-and-embrace-our-differences/

7 ways to help teens appreciate differences. (2020, January 20). Middle Earth. https://middleearthnj.org/2020/01/20/7-ways-to-help-teens-appreciate-differences/

Aboud, F. E., & Doyle, A. B. (1996). Does talk of race foster prejudice or tolerance in children? *Canadian Journal of Behavioural Science / Revue Canadienne Des Sciences Du Comportement, 28*(3), 161–170. https://doi.org/10.1037/0008-400x.28.3.161

Allen, L., & Kelly, B. B. (2015, July 23). *Child development and early learning.* Nih.gov; National Academies

Press (US). https://www.ncbi.nlm.nih.gov/books/NBK310550/

Are you raising a judgmental child? (2018, February 23). Being the Parent. https://www.beingtheparent.com/are-you-raising-a-judgmental-child/

Aron, S. (2020, January 20). *7 ways to help teens appreciate differences.* Middle Earth. https://middleearthnj.org/2020/01/20/7-ways-to-help-teens-appreciate-differences/

Belhap, M. (2016, June 30). *Why diversity exposure is key in early education development.* ISTUDENTglobal. https://i-studentglobal.com/what-to-study/student-lifestyle/why-diversity-exposure-is-important-in-early-education-development/

Borba, M. (2018, June 12). *10 ways to raise a tolerant child.* The Children's Trust. https://www.thechildrenstrust.org/content/10-ways-raise-tolerant-child

Bracken, A. (2021, January 20). *How to raise an activist.* Parents. https://www.parents.com/parenting/better-parenting/advice/how-to-raise-an-activist/

Carnoy, M., & García, E. (2017). Five key trends in U.S. student performance. *Economic Policy Institute.* Economic Policy Institute. https://www.epi.org/publication/five-key-trends-in-u-s-student-performance-progress-by-Blacks-and-hispanics-the-takeoff-of-asians-the-stall-of-non-english-speakers-the-persistence-of-socioeconomic-gaps-and-the-damaging-effect/#epi-toc-14

Cesare, C. (2015). Cultural differences determine when kids learn to play fair. *Nature.* https://doi.org/10.1038/nature.2015.18816

Curry, O. S., Price, M. E., & Price, J. G. (2008). Patience is a virtue: Cooperative people have lower discount rates. *Personality and Individual Differences*, *44*(3), 780–785. https://doi.org/10.1016/j.paid.2007.09.023

Davis, T. (2021, August 2). *How to practice acceptance.* Psychology Today. https://www.psychologytoday.com/us/blog/click-here-happiness/202108/how-practice-acceptance

Fabrega, M. (2019, October 23). *How to practice acceptance.* Daringtolivefully.com. https://daringtolivefully.com/how-to-practice-acceptance

Fraser, J. (2016, February 21). *Why don't kids speak up about bullying?* The Edvocate. https://www.theedadvocate.org/why-dont-kids-speak-up-about-bullying/

García, E. (2020, February 12). *Schools are still segregated, and Black children are paying a price*. Economic Policy Institute. https://www.epi.org/publication/schools-are-still-segregated-and- Black-children-are-paying-a-price/

Hall, K. (2018). *Create a sense of belonging*. Psychology Today.

https://www.psychologytoday.com/us/blog/pieces-mind/201403/create-sense-belonging

How to stop being a judgmental parent. (n.d.). Wellbeing Centre. Retrieved November 12, 2021, from https://www.wellbeingcenter.co/article.php?How-To-Stop-Being-A-Judgmental-Parent-514

Kinzler, K. D., & Spelke, E. S. (2011). Do infants show social preferences for people differing in race? *Cognition*, *119*(1), 1–9. https://doi.org/10.1016/j.cognition.2010.10.019

Kosciw, J. G., Greytak, E. A., Zongrone, A. D., Clark, C. M., & Truong, N. L. (2018). The 2017 national school climate survey: The experiences of lesbian, gay, bisexual, transgender, and queer youth in our nation's schools. GLSEN. https://www.glsen.org/sites/default/files/2019-10/GLSEN-2017-National-School-Climate-Survey-NSCS-Full-Report.pdf

Lease, A. M., & Blake, J. J. (2005). A comparison of majority-race children with and without a minority-race friend. *Social Development*, *14*(1), 20–41. https://doi.org/10.1111/j.1467-9507.2005.00289.x

Mathias, B., & Mary Ann French. (1996). *40 ways to raise a nonracist child.* Harperperennial.

McNamara, C. (2017). *Diversity and inclusion: How to value diverse people and organizations.* Managementhelp.org. https://managementhelp.org/interpersonal/multicultural-diversity.htm

Media, B. T. (n.d.). *Article - diversity: No longer just Black and White.* Business Training Media. Retrieved November 11, 2021, from https://www.businesstrainingmedia.com/culturaldiversityartcile.php

Mendoza-Denton, R. (2011, May 5). *Should we talk to young children about race?* Greater Good. https://greatergood.berkeley.edu/article/item/should_we_talk_to_young_children_about_race

Miller, C. (2019). *The importance of promoting diversity in early childhood programs | the infant crier.* Mi-

Aimh.org. https://infantcrier.mi-aimh.org/the-importance-of-promoting-diversity-in-early-childhood-programs/

Newman, K. M. (2016). *Four reasons to cultivate patience.* Greater Good. https://greatergood.berkeley.edu/article/item/four_reasons_to_cultivate_patience

Pulido-Tobiassen, D., & Gonzalez-Mena, J. (1999). A place to begin: Working with parents on issues of diversity. In *Google Books*. California Tomorrow. https://books.google.com.pk/books/about/A_Place_to_Begin.html?id=-gARAQAAIAAJ&redir_esc=y

R. Comer, D., & E. Sekerka, L. (2014). Taking time for patience in organizations. *Journal of Management Development*, *33*(1), 6–23. https://doi.org/10.1108/jmd-11-2013-0132

Ream, G. L. (2019). What's unique about lesbian, gay, bisexual, and transgender (LGBT) youth and young adult suicides? Findings from the national violent death reporting system. *Journal of Adolescent Health*, *64*(5). https://doi.org/10.1016/j.jadohealth.2018.10.303

Richfield, S. (2019, August 6). *Teach your judgmental child to be open minded.* Healthyplace.com. https://www.healthyplace.com/parenting/the-parent-coach/teach-your-judgmental-child-to-be-open-minded

Rosenthal, L., Earnshaw, V. A., Carroll-Scott, A., Henderson, K. E., Peters, S. M., McCaslin, C., & Ickovics, J. R. (2013). Weight- and race-based bullying: Health associations among urban adolescents. *Journal of Health Psychology*, *20*(4), 401–412. https://doi.org/10.1177/1359105313502567

Saylor, C. F., & Leach, J. B. (2008). Perceived bullying and social support in students accessing special inclusion programming. *Journal of Developmental and Physical Disabilities*, *21*(1), 69–80. https://doi.org/10.1007/s10882-008-9126-4

Schnitker, S. A., & Emmons, R. A. (2007). Patience as a virtue: Religious and psychological perspectives. *Research in the Social Scientific Study of Religion, Volume 18*, *18*, 177–207. https://doi.org/10.1163/ej.9789004158511.i-301.69

Schwabe, J. (2019, October 30). *Develop patience and tolerance*. Practical Widsom. https://medium.com/practical-mind-mastery/develop-patience-and-tolerance-4dce9419f739

Seldin, M., & Yanez, C. (2019). *Student reports of bullying: Results from the 2017 school crime supplement to the national crime victimization survey*. National Center for Education Statistics.

Ten ways to fight hate: A community response guide. (2017, August 14). SPLC Southern Poverty Law Center. https://www.splcenter.org/20170814/ten-ways-fight-hate-community-response-guide

Want to raise empowered kids? Teach advocacy! (n.d.). Doing Good Together™. Retrieved November 12, 2021, from https://www.doinggoodtogether.org/bhf/blog/teach-advocacy

Watkins, D. (2015, April 27). *How school grooms african americans for the underclass.* Aeon. https://aeon.co/essays/how-school-grooms-african-americans-for-the-underclass

Weiss, S. R. (2020, June 11). *Raise your kids to be activists who change the world.* SheKnows. https://www.sheknows.com/feature/children-activists-protests-parents-2272618/

www.ingramcontent.com/pod-product-compliance
Lightning Source LLC
La Vergne TN
LVHW051019080826
845145LV00009B/2697

* 9 7 8 1 9 5 6 0 1 8 2 5 7 *